When Therapy Fails

Mishandling of The Transference

By

Sandra L. Wyllie

This book is dedicated to:

 the Scarecrow, the Tin Man, the Cowardly Lion, and OZ

With love to my sons Alex & Austin

All people's names have been changed for their own
protection.

You won't find home somewhere out there. Home is inside
each one of us, when we allow love to enter us.

Please feel free to contact me at: leeann827@hotmail.com

Table of Contents

He Hit Me

like pelting hail
till I had bumps
raised as braille
and he danced all over them
using his finger as a pen

He hit me
like a flying dart
pierced the bullseye
I, his mark
on his first throw
had me from the go

He hit me
like a bombing blizzard
billowing white dust
blinding me with every gust
till I was swimming in the soup
and then he flew the coop

He hit me
like quicksand
putty in his hand
as I moved
he would expand
and held me tight
into his chambers
and let me sink
like we were strangers

Chapter 1

Goodbye Email

It's not every day that a patient gets abruptly and unilaterally kicked to the curb by their psychologist in an email. This happening after a two-year therapy is almost unheard of. The only reason a therapist might do this is if they feel personally threatened or someone in their family was threatened. But I assure you that this wasn't the case.

Here is the shocking "goodbye email"

Dear Sandy,

After listening to your voicemail message on Saturday, it's clear we are no longer able to work together. I am confident that you will be able to continue your psychotherapy with someone else. I send you all good wishes.

Sincerely,

Dr. Marvel

When I received this email, I was in a state of shock. Having borderline personality disorder, I am used to ending many therapies and relationships this way. It's the coward's way out from having to say things face to face to someone. It's a good way of avoiding conflict and responsibility. I've been in therapy for over sixteen years, and I have never had a therapist end therapy so abruptly, using email as the way to do in a unilateral decision with no discussion with the patient.

I immediately called him back and left two voice
messages on his answering machine to see me for a last
session, which is the professional thing to do. I also wrote
Dr. Marvel –

It is totally unprofessional to end therapy of two years
with a patient via email WITHOUT a last session. I know
you're in a "reactive/protective state", but I am imploring
you NOT to end it like this…. WITHOUT a last session to
discuss things. I KNOW we can work this out. I have
ended therapy countless times like this. I will admit this
is the FIRST time a therapist has done it to me.

Dr. Marvel, you are BETTER than this. PLEASE allow me
my session tomorrow.

Sandy

Hours after the phone messages of my begging him to see
me for a last session and this email he finally called me
back and relented. I had hoped that this meant I had a
chance to clear the air with him. Unfortunately, it didn't.
He had his mind made up before I even got to the
appointment. I went in for my two-thirty session very
nervous and fearful of his rejection. He greeted me with a
tense look. As soon as I sat down, I explained to him that
I was in total shock by his email abruptly ending the
treatment. I said that as a borderline patient I have done
this countless times before to therapists, but this was the
very first time a professional has ever done so with me.

Borderline personality disorder, which is what I have, is characteristic of having extreme fears of abandonment and trouble staying in relationships. To treat a borderline this way is reprehensible.

I was already reeling from my last psychologist who was unethical and had a sexual relationship with me for two years. Now this one was kicking me to the curb.I sat there, threw my pride out the window, and begged him not to end the treatment. I was drinking heavy and needed help. All he said was "I can't." Through my swollen face and streaked tears, I said "you won't". And then he repeated that back to me, confirming the obvious, that he had his mind all made up before I had even entered the door and sat down for the session. He said the phone call was what did it. But he also spilled off a laundry list of the things I did that he didn't like in the last two years.

The phone call was made on the previous Saturday Morning. The reasons leading up to that phone call were many. I had felt that since Dr. Marvel returned from his vacation, he didn't look completely relaxed. When I asked him where he went he wouldn't say. But what he *did* say revealed much. He said that he was dealing with "family matters". It sounded to me that it wasn't a vacation that was totally leisurely, and that there were "family issues".

The other reason that prompted my phone call is because I thought that he wasn't handling the transference well. The patients projected feeling onto the therapist is called transference. The therapist's projected feeling onto the patient is called countertransference. He wasn't handling my feelings of love and sexual longings.

He was either acting defensive (resisting them) or acting dissociative (ignoring them).

A professional is supposed to be able to handle all the feelings the patient has. They are especially trained to do just that.

When a therapist has unresolved issues of their own it can interfere with the therapy. This is a good time for the therapist to get some supervision and/or seek their own individual therapy with their own therapist. I brought these issues up to Dr. Marvel on the phone message, saying he needed supervision because he wasn't handling the transference. I also said that it felt like he was in the beginning stages of burning out.

 For some therapists it is very hard for them to handle their "own stuff" (old wounds from their past). I think Dr. Marvel's pride was badly wounded, when his own patient (me) pointed out what he should have known from his own personal training. It was adding insult to injury when I told him to call his old supervisor from thirty years ago. I was seeing his old supervisor at the same time I was seeing him as well.

I always had more than one therapist, which is highly unusual. But I did this because I could not get all the help I needed from any one of them. I decided to write this book to help other patients notice the warning signs of when a therapist isn't handling their own issues and letting that interfere with the therapy. There were warning signs right from the start that I refused to see.

The end of any relationship is always difficult, especially one that has failed so badly. We cannot allow ourselves to turn bitter and become afraid to trust other people again. Although I will admit, I have much work ahead of me in the department of trust. Dr. Marvel was not the first therapist to harm me from the mishandling of the transference.

I just want to say that as patients, we do NOT have to become the victims at the hands of unstable professionals. There are licensing boards that you can write to in your state if a therapist has become unethical. You can contact a lawyer and talk about your individual situation to see if you can get compensation if you have been badly mishandled by the very person that you sought out to help you. You can take legal action. When you do you will become in control and no longer a helpless person.

In this case I did not seek action because I was already seeing two other psychologists. One I was seeing once a week. The other I was seeing once every few months.

I know that Dr. Marvel would have used that fact against me, saying it was NOT abandonment since I had two other psychologists to turn to. What he did was unprofessional and wrong. I regret not going to the board. I have written formal complaints about other therapists. I am a seasoned patient. I was truly thrown by the immature way Dr. Marvel handled things.

For therapy to work there must be trust between the patient and therapist. It all starts with a healthy therapist who isn't afraid to analyze himself and be in his own therapy.

Remember, the patient is the boss. If you don't like what you are paying for FIRE them. After all, it is the patient's insurance that pays their bills. Don't you ever forget that!

I wanted to share some of my background, so you understand why I was seeking out therapy in the first place. I grew up an only child in Boston with two very psychologically disturbing parents. My father was a paranoid schizophrenic who was in and out of mental hospitals all his life. He was seeing a psychiatrist. A psychiatrist does therapy like a psychologist. The only difference is that a psychiatrist is also a medical doctor and because of that they can write you prescriptions for psychotropic medication.

Schizophrenia is a long-term severe brain disorder involving a breakdown in the relation between thought, emotion, and behavior, leading to faulty perception, inappropriate actions and feelings, withdrawal from reality and personal relationships into fantasy and delusion, and a sense of mental fragmentation.

My father had paranoid delusions where he thought people, we trying to kill him or his family (including me). It was horrifying growing up with a parent that made me fear everyone and trust no one.

What made the situation even worse was that when I got frightened by my father's delusions my mother used to swear at me for making her life harder. She would belittle me, beat me until I bled and call horrific names. I had no siblings to turn to and my friends didn't know the house of hell I lived in. My parents kept a "good front" to the outside world.
Back then people turned the other cheek, teachers, and families alike. No one wanted to deal with this stuff.
I battled severe crippling anxiety all my life. I also had great social phobias that prevented me from attending many family get-togethers. I never could keep a job or a relationship long. However, I am still in a thirty plus marriage with an amazing husband who has supported me through everything. I have two grown children. Alex is my first born. He is twenty-six and living in a special group home for brain damaged children. He has permanent brain damage from meningitis which he got at the tender age of four. My other son Austin, who is twenty-four, is in college double majoring in psychology and public health.

I am writing to share with you how my therapies had failed me and what you can do to spot that if it happens to you. I also write this book so that other professional therapists can see the errors of their own kind.

A therapist's job is first and foremost "to do no harm". It is the Hippocratic Oath that every professional must take to be in this field. Most of them uphold to the high standards put upon them. You could look up those standards yourself. One of those standards is that under no circumstances should a therapist ever engage in sex with a patient. Sex and therapy *NEVER MIX*.

Ironically, I contacted Dr. Marvel because my last therapist had issues with the transference as well. I wrote him a goodbye email (just like Dr. Marvel did with me). I went on Psychology Today's website and looked up psychologists. And that is where I stumbled upon Dr. Marvel's profile. From reading his profile and seeing his picture it appeared he was a very kind and compassionate man.

And so, I had an appointment exactly one week after breaking off the therapy with my former therapist. I didn't miss a beat! The most ironic thing of all in this is that Dr. Marvel was not only in the same town as my other therapist, (he was walking distance from my last psychologist) the sessions were the exact SAME day and exact SAME time as I had with my previous psychologist. At this time as well, I was dating and in a sexual relationship with another psychologist I had done therapy with.

I was also in another long-term therapy with a
psychologist I had known since 2005. I was seeing this
man for forty minutes once a week for free. I was afraid
that Dr. Marvel wouldn't approve of my having two
psychologists at the same time. No one understands that
concept. Most think that having two therapists would
confuse the patient. But this never was the case for me.

Chapter 2

A New Beginning

He wasn't on time. That's the first thing I noticed about Dr. Marvel. While I was "waiting" in his waiting room I noticed all the sculptures on the wall. They had his signature on them. He was an artist! I admired this because I loved to draw and paint birds. My aunt used to be a great painter. My mother hung up her paintings in our house. There was even one of her paintings on the wall above my brass bed as a teenager.

He was an abstract artist. His sculptures were in earth tones, and almost jump out of the frames, like volcano ash. They were made of wire and wood and dried flowers. I knew what he already looked like by his profile on Psychology Today's website, which by the way is a great place to find a therapist. I took one of his cards he had on a table next to the chair I was sitting on. He also had many interesting books on that table about philosophy and death, interesting I thought.

He finally came out from a side door. His office was inside his house, like the previous ones I had been in. I like home offices much better. They are more relaxing and less clinical. You also get to know about the therapist this way. I am always interested in getting to know my therapists in a personal manner.

He was older, in his sixties. I was always looking for a father figure since my dad died when I was thirty-eight years old. I entered the therapy room. I gave him the co-pay and sat down in the only two chairs beside his own he had to offer. His degrees hung on the wall. More of his artwork hung on the wall as well. My eyes darted all around the room, trying to stay focused on the man in front of me.

I gave him some background information about me. I told him I was a poet. He asked me to email him some of my poems. I told him that I was in a torrid affair. But I did not tell him the whole truth about Dean. I lied and told him that Dean was a dentist. I picked "dentist" because as a dentist that would make Dean my doctor and I his patient, which wasn't a total lie. It was just a lie about his profession. I also didn't let on that I was seeing another therapist for free, which happened to be his former supervisor! It's a small world.

I really hate lying. I'm not condoning what I did. I just didn't feel safe enough yet to tell him the whole truth. I needed to build up the trust before I could do that. You should always be completely open and honest with your therapist. If you find that you can't do that then it's time you find a new therapist. And your therapist should be able to handle anything you tell them without reaction or judgement.

The next appointment he arrived late again, and the next one after that, and the one after that as well. I didn't like this at all. I'm a very punctual person. I was paying for a "50 minute" session and he was short-changing me. I already felt short-changed by the therapist I was seeing for free. He only gave me a 40-minute session. He gave all his other patients the typical 50-minute slot. Also, he took a session away from me, telling me he had to drive his daughter to basketball practice. Then I found out he lied when I saw another patient go in (at what used to be my time slot) as I was leaving. I threatened him with the board over this but later rescinded.

 I kept sweeping "the time" under the rug, telling myself that he was only a few minutes late. Other than tardiness I felt he listened well, was empathic, and that maybe, just maybe I could trust him.

Then I received my new health card in the mail. I noticed that my co-pay had gone up by five dollars. Now I was paying him an extra five dollars a week and not getting my full time of 50 minutes. This irked me even more. Yet I was afraid to bring it up to him in the session. I didn't want to make waves and create any tension with yet another therapist.

The final straw came when I saw a young blonde patient leave his office at twenty-four past the hour. His sessions ran on the half-hour. He always ended mine a minute early at three-nineteen. And he always started a few minutes late. So instead of two-thirty, he would start at two-thirty-two or three. When I saw the young woman coming out four minutes after the session should have ended for her, I got extremely jealous.

I didn't think it was fair. I was fifty-two, not nearly as young or as pretty.

The next session I broached the subject of his tardiness. He was very indignant and quite defensive about it. He said, "I have things to do." I couldn't believe this coming from a professional. I told him it was his job, and that when you have a job you have a responsibility to be on time. He said that his other patients never complained. I noticed that the clocks in his office weren't set to the right time as well. I pointed this out to him. He acted as if I was being demanding by expecting him to be on time and upholding the fifty-minute session.

Then he started complaining about insurance only paying for forty-five minutes. I said if that was the case why didn't he change the sessions to forty-five-minute time slots. He then bitterly said that he does fifty minutes sessions. I had to go to one session carrying a huge wooden numbered "50" in my hands that I painted bright orange. During that session he asked, "Is that your age?" I said "NO", "it's the time you're supposed to give me during my sessions." Really, I can't believe the lengths I had to go through just to get his time that MY MONEY was paying him for!

As a patient and especially as a person with human dignity I deserve respect. Eventually, after many sessions of butting heads with this man he DID start coming to the sessions on time. I asked him if he was like this in his past. He told me as a kid he would always make his father wait for him when he came to pick him up after school. I told him that his father should have just let him find his own way home and left him there.

That would have taught him to treat people with respect. I thought that after a few months it was time to come clean about my seeing another therapist for free and my sexual relationship with my former psychologist. At that time, I was also going to couples therapy with Dean (my lover/former psychologist) and Dr. Love (the one who was seeing me for free). As it turned out Dr. Love used to be Dr. Marvel's supervisor over thirty years ago.

He seemed not to be bothered by this new information. So, I thought we were starting to do well together. I also noticed during this time that he would keep moving my Tuesday session to Wednesdays, which was fine with me. As a writer I can be very flexible with my schedule. It was a little odd though that he always had to be out of the office the same time on Tuesdays. But much larger things were starting to happen to me currently.

At this time, I ended the unethical/sexual relationship with my former psychologist, Dean. I did indeed tell Dr. Marvel the whole sordid details. It really helped to unload it all on Dr. Marvel. He would occasionally "slip" and come in late again. And again, I would stand up for myself. Let me just say that it's hard for a person to change, including your therapist. It was in his nature to be perpetually late. He was going against his nature by being punctual. The next few sessions he came in early. And he fixed all his clocks to the right time. He really was trying. And I truly appreciated him for it.

One day Dr. Marvel called and left a message on my cell asking to switch my Tuesday slot *again* to Wednesday. I called him back saying that it was fine, but that I was starting to get concerned about why he was always out of the office at this time on Tuesdays.

So, when I came in for the next session, which was on a Wednesday I asked him directly what was going on and that, I was very worried about it.

He told me he had a bad heart and that most likely he would require surgery. And that he might possibly be needing the surgery this summer. He said he would be out for six weeks if he did. He said that he would have "railroad track" scars down his chest from the surgery and that he would feel like he's been hit "by a Mack truck" for a long time afterwards.

I was feeling closer to Dr. Marvel after he told me this. I started seeing him as a person, just like myself who was vulnerable. I also started worrying about him a lot. I thought of him as Oz from the Wizard of Oz. He tried to show a brave/courageous face "on the screen" but was just a very insecure man who didn't have any answers and was searching himself for them.

I always related to the character "Dorothy" from the Wizard of Oz, looking for "home", whatever that was. But I've finally learned that "home" is NOT a place, but a feeling of wholeness that you must find within yourself. No one can bring you home. And not even the great Oz, Dr. Marvel would get me there. Some people search a lifetime looking for home, and then die alone without ever really finding it.

The more I worried about Dr. Marvel because of his heart condition I started having these fantasies of him having prostate cancer. I simply didn't know why this was happening to me. But I was so consumed by these thoughts that I had to bring it up in the session. So, the next session I decided to broach the subject with him. Though I knew it would be very difficult to tell my psychologist that I had thoughts that he had cancer, of any kind. So, when I came to the next session, I told him that I had these thoughts. Then I broke down and told him that I had envisioned him with prostate cancer. To my astonishment he said to me "I have it." I almost died! How could I have possibly known? I think I felt deeply enmeshed within this man. As far as his cancer was concerned, it probably wasn't anything he would ever die of. It was at the very beginning stage and had not spread. The doctors would just keep an eye on it. But there was no need for surgery.

For the first time, I was feeling some tendrils of love for Dr. Marvel. I wrote this poem, among many for him:

"Your Face"

If your face was the wind
your whisper would be a cool breeze.
If your face was the moon
your cheeks would be velvet, sweet cream.
If your face was the rain
your nose would blow lavender mist.
If your face was the sun
your lips would have me sun-kissed.

If your face was a star
your eyes would be a kaleidoscope of blooming colors.
And each freckle on your face
would be a distant planet
from another galaxy.
Your ears would be a canal
that would carry all my hopes and dreams.
Each time I look into your face
that is what I see.

By nature, I'm a theatrical person. My grandmother was a singer/dancer in vaudeville. And my mother was a singer at a piano bar. So naturally this started to emerge in my therapy with Dr. Marvel. The first session I ever dressed up for him I came in as an extraterrestrial. I bought an all-green one-piece body suit at Party City. And I also made these antennas that I painted green and wore them on top of my head.

When I walked in, he thought I was a leprechaun! Well, I was all in green! I didn't have anything but a bra and panties underneath this "painted on" green suit, so I was very self-conscious when I left. You could see every curve of my ass! Dr. Marvel told me that he was from "another place" as well. That's when I truly felt one with this man. He strongly believed in reincarnation and that our spirit lives out many lives. I believe that the spirit of a deceased person can enter another form, such a butterfly.

Because of this intense closeness that I was now experiencing parts of myself started emerging inside of the therapy and outside of it as well. I started drawing again. But this time I hung up all my artwork all over my house, just like I had seen Dr. Marvel do in his office. I started writing more books, because Dr. Marvel was also a writer like myself and had published books on the market. And I became more spiritual because of him as well. He was starting to change my life.

One of sessions I brought in all my childhood memorabilia, including my first baby shoes, my christening dress and bonnet, and an old porcelain lamb figurine which held flowers. I brought in pictures of my parents and family. In one of those pictures my mother was dressed in a white dress with black trim. I spent the previous Saturday afternoon looking in every store that resembled that dress. After countless hours and searching many stores, I finally found a dress that looked like that in my size!

I also was wearing my hair like her, piled high atop my head like a beehive. Most people said I looked just like my mother when she was alive. I always hated my mother because she was a very caustic and abusive woman, but for this one session, I wanted to be her. When he looked at the pictures, he didn't put it together. I had to tell him. He also seemed a little irritated by what he called "my props."

Currently, he was also getting annoyed by my constant barrage of emails. I write poems every day and send them to various people. Dr. Marvel was one of them. I also analyzed most of the sessions I had with him. I would send him emails after the session titled "Today's Session." I would often have more thoughts about my true feelings when I wasn't in the therapy room. He told me that he wasn't reading my emails. This felt crushing to me. Writing was like breathing to me. All my other therapists read my emails. It felt like a rejection of who I was and my feelings as well. The problems with emails would always emerge between us until the bitter end.

Chapter 3

A Breakthrough

During this time, I started developing a lot of sexual fantasies about Dr. Marvel. Yet I didn't have the nerve to tell him quite yet. It is perfectly normal for a patient to have sexual feelings and attraction for their therapist. In therapy all your feelings will be projected onto the therapist. It is the professional role of the therapist to hold your feelings in a safe place and not react to them. Here is a poem I wrote about one of those fantasies:

"I Wonder What It Would Feel Like with You"

I love it when your eyes and eyebrows
come together when you're trying to make me laugh.
I wonder what it would feel like with you
if we were washing each other in a sudsy, bubble bath.

I love it when your chest rises and falls
when you're getting worked up about something I said.
I wonder what it would feel like with you
if we were lying in each other's arms, naked in bed.

I love it when you're telling me some quote
from an old Woody Allen movie.
I wonder what it would feel like with you
if we were feeding each other,
licking the sauce off your lips, two star-crossed lovers
embraced in a passionate kiss.

On one occasion I decided I wanted to tape all my feelings onto balloons. I went to the dollar store and bought about a dozen balloons. On each one I wrote in marker a feeling, like sadness, anger, passion, rage, jealousy, etc…..
I also bought weights for each of the twelve balloons so that they wouldn't just float to the ceiling in his office.

I came a few minutes early for the session to "set this up". He always had the door to his office open, so it was easy for me just to walk right in. I guess it took a lot longer than I expected because he came out of the door that connected his home to his office. As I heard him approach, I asked if he could "wait outside his office". He jokingly said, "you're late". I think he was poking fun of all the times he made me wait for the session, when this time I was the one detaining the session.

I will admit he was very accommodating in waiting outside his own office without even knowing what I was doing. When he entered, after I had finished "setting up" there were balloons scattered over every square inch of his office, with all my feelings written on them. He made his way through the maze to his chair. And I made my way to my chair. I was given him "a visual presentation" of many of my deepest feelings. They hung by a string attached to a weight. It was a very deep session for me, being able to express myself like this and see my feelings spelled out visually on all the balloons. What was even more freeing is after I left the session, I drove a little way to a nearby school and released each balloon out the car window. I sat in the car and watched each balloon fly high in the air carrying each one of my emotions, such catharsis.

I knew that Dr. Marvel's birthday was coming up because I had looked it up on the internet. I wanted to make him something special, a homemade gift. I looked up a lot of information on him through various websites. He was a very private man. He wouldn't share many personal details of his life. What I did was take a canvas and painted it a cool bronze color. Then I made three-D images of items that represented is life, in a collage form. I made a three-D petite copy of his book by copying the cover page and reducing it down to size. I then taped this over a tiny matchbox.

I looked up his college and made a logo of that out of wood and painted it. I did things liked that to personalize this collage just for him. I also made him a home-made card telling him that he has been a great inspiration to me and that I love him. And I truly did. We had our share of butting heads, but who doesn't in any deep relationship

Then out of the blue during one of my sessions Dr. Marvel said, "isn't it time we talked about your mother?" I thought this was a bold move. I told him during all my years of therapy with various therapists that I never really talked about her. I said that he would need a pic-axe to break through all my resistance. On the way home from that session, I started thinking about what Dr. Marvel said. Of course, my creative juices started "kicking in".

I ordered a fake pic-axe and a lump of real coal that came in a beautiful light blue box with a white bow on the top of it. The box looked like it came directly out of Tiffany's. I thought of Dr. Marvel as the coal miner going into the dark tunnels of my mind, searching, and probing with his pic-axe, little by little chipping away at me. When I came into the next session, I handed him both the pic-axe and the blue box which contained the coal.

He laid the pic-axe on the table behind him and opened the box. He said "it's coal" I explained what the meaning behind my bringing in these things was. He took one look at me, made one fell swoop right out of his chair to the table behind him, picked up the pic-axe, handed it to me and said, "start chipping away". I sat startled and frightened and said to him "I don't know where to begin; I need help." Ironically, I looked like a little girl in this session. I had my long hair divided into two ponytails that framed my face. I had on a purple striped shirt that looked like a ten-year-old might wear.

Dr. Marvel then told me to remember something about my mother. I sat and tried, for his sake more than mine. I think I wanted to please him. But I also knew that it was important work for myself to be able to do this. A song was coming in my head. I said that I remembered a song. He asked what song and what the words were. I tried harder and remembered it was Helen Reddy's "You and Me against the World." At this point I jumped into the other chair in his office. Switching chairs is something I frequently did when I was anxious.

He pressured me to remember the words of the song. I told him that I would look them up and email it to him. He replied, "I won't read it." In fact, he complained quite often about all my daily emails and how he was not reading them. But I, the eternally optimist kept on sending them anyway. I tried hard and started coming out with more of the lyrics. As I did, I started welling up with tears. It was the very first time in my life that I had soft and tender feelings for my mother instead of the deep-seated hatred that I usually carried around with me.

At the end of the session, I looked deeply into his eyes and thanked him. I also asked him if I could have a hug. No sooner had I asked than his arms spread open wide, taking all of me into them. It was a moment I will never forget for the rest of my life. I would have a lot of these "unforgettable moments" with him. I went home after the session and looked up the words to the song. I made a copy of the lyrics and brought them into my next session. I gave them to Dr. Marvel. He read them silently. He saw that it was a love song sung by a mother to her child. He asked if my mother ever sang that song to me. I told him that I didn't remember because I had a lot of suppressed memories because of her severe abuse. I just knew that that song had significance in our relationship. Dr. Marvel asked to keep the paper with the lyrics on it. I told him that he could.

"You and Me Against the World"

You and me against the world,
Sometimes it seems like you and me against the world,
When all the others turn their backs and walked away,
You can count on me to stay.
Remember when the circus came to town
How you were frightened by the clown,
Wasn't it nice to be around someone that you knew,
Someone who was big and strong and looking out for
You and me against the world,
Sometimes it seems like you and me against the world
And for all the times we've cried I always felt that
God was on our side.
And when one of us is gone,
And one of us is left to carry on,
Then remembering will have to do,
Our memories alone will get us through
Think about the days of me and you,
Of you and me against the world.

When I hear this song, I cry and feel like a little girl all
over again. My mother died in November of 2003, my
father merely three months after her in February of 2004.

On another session I came dressed up as a clown. Again, this time, I hid behind his office door, holding a flower in my hand. My nose and cheeks were painted red with make-up artist's paint. I had on big balloon pink pants with white polka-dots. And I was wearing a long-haired violet wig. On top of my head, I had a black bowl hat with pink polka-dots on it. Around my neck was a bright big pink bowtie. Yup, there was no mistaken me for a clown.

When he came in, he literally knocked the door right into my big bopper of a nozzle! He didn't know that I was directly behind it! I extended my arm, after my recovery and handed him the carnation. Then I turned around and sat down. I think he might have laughed. I saw a smile curl up on the edge of his somber lips.

The next session was really a meaningful one to me. I dressed up as Dorothy from the Wizard of Oz. The Wizard of Oz had always been my favorite movie because I was always searching for brains, courage, a heart, and a home. And I continue to search for them to this day. I also made Dr. Marvel another home-made gift. I took a Styrofoam oval egg and painted it to look like the balloon that Dorothy and Oz climb into at the end of the movie. I tied the Styrofoam egg with thread to a small basket I picked up at the thrift store. I also cut out a picture I printed up of both Dorothy and Oz and glued them into the basket. It came out looking good. Dr. Marvel was impressed because he kept looking at it the whole session. His eyes would dart over to it every now and then during our conversation.

I looked like Dorothy too! I ordered the costume from Amazon, including the ruby shoes. I did not have a little dog to use as Toto though. I do remember one session when Dr. Marvel was dog-sitting for his son's dog while he was away. Dr. Marvel brought the dog into the session. He was large, thin brown dog. I don't know what breed he was. It turned out to be an enjoyable session with the dog constantly trying to get my attention while I was trying to hold a conversation through the dog's eager antics!

The next session that I dressed up for didn't go over well at all. I dressed up like a jockey. I had the white tight cropped riding pants, tugged into black riding boots and the helmet. I also came in with a riding crop, the kind that the jockey uses to hit the horse with. In playful fun I attached the co-pay to the crop with a paperclip. Dr. Marvel thought that it was very condescending of me to do this. I also brought him in a horseshoe. I guess the reason I dressed up as the jockey was because I saw Dr. Marvel as "the horse" that I was going to ride. I haven't analyzed this one totally. Maybe there was some underline domineering fix inside of this for me. But Dr. Marvel was not amused and it kind of turned into a sour session.

 And then things started taking a turn for the worse. I was feeling very anxious all the time. One session I had a very bad panic attack upon arriving to his office. It all started when the road that went to his house was closed because they were repairing the street. I got lost because I don't know the streets in his neighborhood. When one street was closed and there were no detour signs to find my way I panicked and got lost.

I called my husband at work and asked for his help, which is something I usually do. I have no sense of direction in the first place, plus I hate driving.
He told me an alternative way. But unfortunately, that way would take much longer, and I did not allow for the time when I left. Of course, how could I predict the road leading straight to his house would be closed? I started driving fast to make up for the lost time, even though I called him telling him that I would be late. He was nice on the phone. He said to me "do whatever you need to do."

I was gunning it doing about fifty in a twenty-five-mile zone. A teenage girl started making motions with her arms for me to slow down. When I got to his house, I was over ten minutes late, ten minutes that I would lose from my session. I was all out of breath and wound up tighter than a fishing coil. I opened my mouth, but the words just simply could not come out. He just sat there not knowing what to do. I told him that I needed air and then ran out of the therapy room, right out his front door into his lawn. I bent down and picked up a leaf that was on the ground. I took a few moments and then returned to his office holding onto that leaf.

I held onto that leaf, twirling it in my hand for the whole session. Here is a poem I wrote about that session.

"I Didn't Pluck It; It Had Fallen"

A young girl with her dog is frantically flapping
her arm up and down.
Like a bullet shot out of the head of a barrel.
For Christ's sake slow down!!
I didn't really mean to do any harm.
But I can't get past this feeling.
I'm a wire pulled tautly on the line,
wrapped around myself and reeling,
but pretending to be fine.

Instead of naturally breathing in
I'm violently choking on the air.
I finally arrived very late at his house
He's calmly sitting undisturbed in his easy chair.
I try to get out the poison
that's been buried deep inside my chest.
I pace the room looking for any word to find.
Even though I'm doing my best,
I'm still in quite a bind.

But how does one describe rape?
And that of a little child, for Christ's sake!
Outside I took a leaf that was lying on his lawn.
I'm sure he thinks that I'm a flake,
even though I'm pretending that I'm not.
Gently in my hand I held the tawny, little leaf.
I didn't pluck it; it had fallen.
I swear; I'm not a thief.

Chapter 4

Dean's Death

At this point in my therapy, it had been over a year since I broke up with Dean (my former psychologist). During a lot of this therapy with Dr. Marvel I discussed the unethical/sexual relationship that I had with him and its impact on me. So, it wasn't unusual that I brought him up again during this session. Only this time Dr. Marvel's face twisted and contorted into this pained expression. He quietly said softly to me "I have some bad news for you." I almost didn't want to hear it. I asked him if it was somebody I knew. He nodded. He asked me if I wanted him to tell me or wait until I heard it on my own.

I reluctantly agreed that he should tell me. He said, "Dean died." I sat there expressionless, asking if, he was sure. He really didn't know his last name, only his first. And he certainly didn't know what he looked like. He said he was sure. I said repeatedly "I don't believe it." Then I asked how he found out. He told me that he saw it in the morning paper. I told him to go get the paper, as seeing would surely be believing. But I suspected that he had to be wrong.

He went inside his home and came back with the obituary in his hand. I took one look at it and sure enough it was Dean, right there, *his picture, his name.* I STILL could not believe it. I took it from his hand and said, "that's him." I then got up and started pacing back and forth in his office, all the while holding the obituary and crying out at the same time "I can't believe it."

It felt like somebody just told me that I had cancer. I was in the denial state. I thanked Dr. Marvel for telling me. He looked relieved. He said that he wasn't sure it was a good thing to tell me. But at least I could express some of my headache from the news with him.

I left that session taking the obituary with me. I called a couple of other psychologists that knew Dean to let them know. I called a couple of my friends as well. I even talked to a very good friend of Dean's. I told her. She didn't know herself. And she had been friends with him for over thirty years. I told my husband. He was as shocked as I was. I even told my son who knew of the affair.

The next session I had with Dr. Marvel I asked him if he was at an art show in Boston a couple of years ago. I could have sworn that Dean and I walked right by him. He said that he was. Then I remembered him sitting there and that room, surrounded by all his sculptures. I thought that if someone with a crystal ball could tell me back then that the man selling the artwork would become my next shrink and that he would be the one to tell me that Dean had died I simply wouldn't have believed them. It felt like Dr. Marvel was an omen.

I started taking up drinking again, this time every day. Before Dr. Marvel had given me the news about Dean, I had cut way back to only drinking twice a week, and not even that much on those days. But now, I fell right back on my old crutch again. Somehow though, through all of this I felt exceptionally close to Dr. Marvel. I suppose because he was the one to break the news to me, and because it felt like fate that brought us together.

It was a bad summer. Every weekend it happened to rain. So, I never got a chance to go to the beach. This one Saturday it looked like the rain might hold off. Andrew, (my husband) and I decided to wing it and go for it. The beach was always "my place." I'm under the water sign of cancer and feel at peace and one with the ocean. When we got there the rain held off. But it was freezing cold and very cloudy. I ordered a lobster roll, which came packed with a ton of fries. I was just too filled up after eating the lobster to eat the fries. So, I packed them in my bag and headed for the sand.

I rolled out my large blue blanket that I always take with me, put on my jacket, and just sat and looked out over the ocean. I noticed that that day the beach was even more mobbed with seagulls than usual. One of them had what looked like a broken leg. He was straggly, dirty, and sick looking. There was another that looked as proud and bold as a bald eagle. I took out my fries and started nibbling on them, not out of hunger, but more out of boredom.

As I was sitting on my blanket, munching my fries the seagulls surrounded me on all sides looking mightily hungry. I decided to throw them a few fries. The big bold one started "fighting off" the other ones to get all the fries. I wanted to be fair. So, I threw the fries to the other ones too, especially the one with the broken leg. He looked thin. I wrote a poem about my experience with these birds.

"The Seagulls And I"

Yesterday I sat on my blue blanket
on a very rocky shore,
and stared out toward the ocean,
watching the seagull's soar.
It was very cold and cloudy
on this grey Saturday afternoon.
I threw some of my leftover fries to the seagulls.
One was acting like a goon,
making so much noise,
thrusting out his bright, white chest like big baboon.

One of the grey ones was limping.
He had a broken leg. So, he teetered and swayed.
But he came right up upon my blanket.
He wasn't one bit afraid.
I started getting hungry, so I joined in their feast.
We were all eating fries, the seagulls and I,
on a very empty beach.
I'd be telling you a lie
If I told you I wasn't disappointed
that the sun played hide and seek.

But the lack of better weather
didn't prevent me from having fun.
Because I discovered that happiness depends
not upon the warmth of the sun,
but rather, a shared meal among my feathered friends,
The seagulls and I.
As I turned and left, I was sad to say goodbye.

I combed the beach on my next excursion there and again it wasn't a very good beach day. The fog that day was as thick as pea soup. I decided to look for shells. I love collecting shells. But this time I decided to make something special with them. I started putting the arrangement together. As I was doing this, the lifeguard, (who happened to look like my son's age) came up to me. He said that I was very creative and that what I put together looked so good that I could sell it! Wow! This did well for my ego.

It helped me to heal. But I knew that I wanted to give my figure to Dr. Marvel. When I went to my next session, I presented it to him. Do you know what his first words were? "You used a lot of glue on this." I did, but that's not the point. I put a lot of effort into making that for him. And the first thing he noticed about it was how much glue I had used. Things were not going so well between us. I felt like he just didn't "get me". And that's not a good thing when you don't feel understood by your therapist. He didn't appreciate my poetry or my creativity. He refused to read my emails, which mainly consisted of my poetry.

I thought for the next session I should broach the things that bothered me in the therapy. I wrote them down on a piece of paper because I easily forget these days, with getting older and my drinking frying out my brain. To use some levity and be "playful" about it I printed up an employee evaluation form from the internet and filled it out about Dr. Marvel.

I came into the next session and handed the paper to him. He took one look at it and put it down. He was quite angry and upset. He said, "You're not my boss." Actually, this is not true. It was my insurance money paying him. I told him that I needed to discuss some of the things that he was doing that were bothering me. But although I did try talking to him, he got very defensive. He did admit to me though, that the evaluation form hurt his feelings. After he told me this, I got up took the paper and ripped it up and threw it in his waste basket. He then looked at me squarely and asked, "did you do that to say "so there" or because I told you I was hurt?" I replied "both." He then said with a big grin "honest."

There was another session when I came into his office to "check the clocks" because he was always late. I wanted to make sure we were "keeping the same time". He was livid. He told me "I don't like you holding me accountable." There were other times as well when I needed to talk about my feelings and Dr. Marvel would just "shut down" on me.

One time I knew from the minute that I walked into the door that he didn't look right. I asked him what was wrong. But he refused to tell me, even though it was evident that he wasn't himself. I wasted my entire session trying to get out of him what the problem was. He refused to tell me until the next session that he was having chest pain. Well, at least we didn't waste two sessions on it. A therapist "withholding" and NOT self-disclosing can be damaging at times. If the patient notices something about you, acknowledge it.

The next struggle I started having with Dr. Marvel is that I started writing poems about my sexual fantasies of him. It is perfectly normal for a patient to have sexual fantasies of their therapist. The therapist is supposed to know how to handle them and to never act out on them. Dr. Marvel made me feel dirty, just like my mother did when I was a child. He told me he didn't want me to send him any more emails. I said that I would have to look for another therapist because writing was like breathing to me. We finally came to an agreement that he would read my emails if I didn't have any sexual content in them.

I thought this was a fair compromise. But still, I couldn't really discuss any of the feelings I had for him. He was very dismissive of that. I thought it wasn't necessary for my therapy to talk about the sexual ones, if I could talk about other ones, I would be ok with that. It did take away some of my freedom of expression.

But I did have to wonder why poems like this highly offended him, especially when they were about someone else. I wrote a very sexually graphic email about Dean's short. Dr. Maverick took it personally and thought that I was talking about him. But how could I possibly be? I didn't know Dr. Marvel intimately.

This was one of the graphic poems I sent about Dean:

"His Shorts"

They hung on the doorknob.
He didn't wear underwear.
Black, sweat, ejaculate,
Piss and pubic hair
I would snuggle them.
Inhale all his scent.
He didn't wash them.
Oh, how they were succulent!
Everything him
was inside the loose knit cloth.
I drank it up
like it was broth.
Got drunk on it
like it was gin,
wearing a foolish
child-like grin.

Chapter 5

Tug Of War

Dr. Marvel and I were having many struggles I thought it would be appropriate to bring in my next prop. I had to go to Home Depot to get the exact kind of thick and heavy rope that I needed. I wanted the rope to look like it could be used in a real person-to-person tug of war. I entered Dr. Marvel's office and placed one end of the rope on his chair and the other end on my chair. When he walked in, he asked "what's this?" I told him to take one end of it. And I took the other end and then we both "tugged on the rope."

I told him that the therapy with him was like having a tug of war. He often would get defensive with me and put a wall where he shut out his feelings. I desperately wanted to tear down every wall he ever erected. And it would hurt me when I couldn't break them down. Despite all of this I grew to love him more and more. I carried a picture of him around with me that I got off the internet.

Dr. Marvel never liked the idea of me having two therapists, but he went along with it. I was very scared to ask Dr. Marvel if he would cover for my other therapist when he was on vacation. So instead, I made an appointment with someone else (a former psychologist who also let go of me over transference issues) and told Dr. Marvel about it. Then I told him that I was afraid of his rejecting me if I had asked him to take on another session. I said, "I should have asked you". He told me "Should haves don't count."

But he did agree to do it. So, I was happy when my other therapist came back from his vacation, I asked Dr. Marvel if I could keep seeing him twice a week. And to my surprise, he complied. It seemed to be going well for the next several sessions. At last Dr. Marvel, himself told me that he was taking his own vacation that would last two weeks. That was hard to accept because I was deeply in love with him at this point. I knew I would miss him intensely. I told Dr. Marvel right before he left how much I was going to miss him and sent him this poem:

"When You're Gone"

When you're gone
I'm going to miss you
like a hungry baby misses suckling on
their momma's full, milky breast.
Like the honeybee would miss collecting
the sugar-rich nectar from a flower.
Like a scorching drought without suspecting
a rain shower.

When you're gone
I'm going to miss you
like the dark night misses the first light of dawn.
Like a burning fever
misses a cool, wet cloth.
Like a sick, tired man coming home
without a bowl of freshly made broth.

When you're gone
I'm going to miss you
like a conductor of an orchestra without his baton.
Like a blank, empty piece of paper
without a word or a note.
Like a cadaver's still heart
can no longer devote
any more love, without pulsing, fresh blood.

He never acknowledged my feelings of missing him, my feelings of love, or the erotic transference that I was having. I don't know what was going on for him. But I kept thinking something just wasn't right. When he went away, I saw my old psychologist for those two weeks. I discussed my feelings for Dr. Marvel with him, including the sexual fantasies in vivid detail. I had this sexual fantasy (that I never told Dr. Marvel) of him having sex with two young women in their twenties.

One of the women was laying on her back on his desk, while he was standing over her, fucking her brains out. Her legs were bent, and he was holding onto them as he was pounding the hell away deep inside of her. The other woman was on her knees beside Dr. Marvel looking, eager and waiting. He then pulls his stiff erection out of the woman on her back and thrusts it deeply into the mouth of the eager woman on her knees next to him. Then he explodes in the woman's mouth while the other woman on her back watches.

I never fully engaged in all my sexual fantasies. I got married extremely young to my first boyfriend. And I was raised with a very frigid mother who hated sex. She used to call me a whore, slut, and cocksucker just because I masturbated, even when I was STILL a virgin!!

During Dr. Marvel's vacation, I sent him emails daily counting down the day that I would see him again. He would get emails from me with the subject heading like this: "9 MORE DAYS!" "8 MORE DAYS" "I MISS YOU LIKE CRAZY!!!!!!!" Writing him while he was away seemed to help a little. I even cut back on my drinking because he told me that he would continue to see me twice a week. I started feeling hopeful until the floor dropped out from beneath my feet.

The day had finally arrived when I would see Marvel!! I had printed up more pictures of him from his Facebook page. He had an album of pictures from a wedding he went to in August. In one of the pictures, I saw him kneeling beside a belly dancer. I was extremely jealous when I saw how close he was to her in the picture, and how his eyes were all over her. I wanted his eyes to be all over me instead. I wasn't sure I should bring this up to him or not.

When he first came out, he did not look happy at all. I started getting nervous. The first thing I said after he sat down was that I missed him. He said: "Let me go first." It looked like he had something very important to tell me. He started off by telling me how emotionally draining it was receiving all my emails of love/longing when he was on a vacation with his family. He told me that he didn't read them until he came back.

I asked him how it could possibly be "draining to him" when he didn't even read them. He just kept restating that he was on vacation with his family. Then he said, "I don't want to be your muse; I don't want you to have loving feelings for me." He said this without any emotion at all. I wondered to myself why he couldn't handle my loving feelings. Maybe I stirred up something deep inside of him that he had repressed.

I asked him where he went on his vacation, just to make casual talk and bring some levity to what was becoming a grave situation, the very first day he came back. He answered: "I was taking care of family matters." He also mentioned that he felt jet-lagged. I got the feeling that there was more to his vacation than some R&R. I promised him that I wouldn't write him anymore when he went on vacation, since it seemed very upsetting to him.

I then took out the picture of him and the belly dancer. He grew even more upset that I was looking on his Facebook page. I told him that anyone can look on someone's Facebook unless they have filters, only allowing access to family and friends, which he clearly didn't have. Yet he got very angry at me for doing this and acted like I hacked into his account. I'm a curious person by nature. I always like to see pictures of people's families. That is why I joined Facebook to begin with. I see former people that I worked with get married, have children, and even suffer from cancer that I would never even have known otherwise.

He looked haggard as well. Something felt different. And I started really worrying about him. I wrote this email to him about these worries that had me up all night consumed by them.

Dr. Marvel,

Was up last night worried about you. Something doesn't feel right within you. I'm worried that something is going on. You just got back from "what was supposed to be a vacation" and you look like you could use another one. I could have sworn I saw a tear in your eye yesterday when we talked about heat/rage and that through death we escape it. I think something resonated in that for you. I hope you're up for talking about this on Friday.

"Holding Back"

He's holding back desire.
Once he could feel.
Scared to feel the fire,
that he may burn.
Holding back the child,
the one who yearns.
He's holding back his rage.
He's been wronged.
It seems so natural to him.
He's done it so long.

He's holding back his wants.
He has needs.
He always took on the role,
the one to please.
He's holding back the tears,
through his firm grip.
Though, I swear to God,
I thought I saw it slip.
His passion coming out
in his craft.
His art is where his heart is at.
I want to reach out to him,
and touch his soul.
I want to tell the man
Please "Let Go"

When the next session came it was more of the same
thing. I tried to talk about my feelings and my worries,
but he kept his walls up very high and became more and
more defensive. I was starting to think that he needed
help in managing his transference and the start of what I
thought looked like a "burnout." Sometimes it's hard for a
therapist to see they are burnt out when they are in the
middle of it. They try to deny it. I thought that might be
the case here with Dr. Marvel. I thought hard about what
I should do to try to help him. I finally came up with the
idea that he should get some consultation, another
professional with whom he could discuss these issues that
he was grappling with.

Feeling this way, I left him a phone message asking Dr. Marvel to call his old supervisor who happened to also be the psychologist that I was seeing for free. This man had been doing therapy for over forty years. He gave couple's therapy to Dean and me. I had been in analysis for two years with him. He had seen me at my worse. He has even seen me completely naked! I stripped for him during one of my sessions and he wrote a paper about it.

That one phone call and that one message would be the fatal mistake to end the therapy with Dr. Marvel. How could I possibly know how much one small phone call, which was non-threatening could provoke him to end a two-year therapy unilaterally in an email?

When I received the email, I was in total shock. I called him back and begged him to give me a last session. I left a couple messages like that crying and pleading on the phone, along with an email. I could NOT believe this was happening. Eventually, after hours he called me back telling me to come at my appointed day and time. I felt at least hopeful that he would see. But I started to have severe panic attacks worrying about the session. I was worried that I was going to hit "his wall" again and that he was "just going through the motions."

I sent him this email before the fated final session:

Dr. Marvel - I've been in your shoes countless times
running away from the therapy. I'm glad you decided to
meet with me today. I really can empathize from my own
experience of doing exactly what you did in that email.
WE CAN GET THROUGH THIS!

" The Monsters Under Your Bed"

The monsters under your bed
are really ones in your head.
Making you want to run
like the flying nun.
In running they grow larger.
They always have a built-in charger.
Making you feel like a child,
one that's been exiled,
until you totally shut down.
Inside yourself you drown.
All the pains from the past
that you thought had surely passed
have suddenly emerged.
And so, you feel urged
to push them all back.
You're feeling under attack.
They stay hidden under your bed.
At least they're out of your head
For now..........
anyhow.
But they're steadfast,
until you face them at last.

Chapter 6

The Final Farewell

Before I even went into that final session with Dr. Marvel, I called my other psychologist and he made me feel hopeful. He said that he thought that it is likely that Dr. Marvel had an open mind by allowing me to come in. Then I called my husband as well because I was a nervous wreck about this appointment. Both my husband and my other psychologist told me that it was up to me to convince him to keep me. No matter how hurt and abandoned I felt there would be no yelling or name-calling.

When I got there, I was clearly shaken. Never had this ever happened to me. All my old childhood wounds came clearly to the surface. I felt like I was having post-traumatic stress disorder when you relive an old wound of the past in the present. I took my seat and told him that I was in complete shock and deeply hurt by his email. I begged him to give me a second chance. I cried and pleaded for him not to abandon me. It was all in vain. He just told me "He can't." He mentioned the employee evaluation, the sexual fantasies, looking at his Facebook page. It felt like he was keeping a tally of all the things that I did that he didn't like.

These final words haunted me "you said you'd let me go." I sat there crying, begging, and pleading. It felt like he had a heart of stone. But deep inside I knew that I had to let him go, even though I didn't want to.

I walked out of his office in a daze. I went home and made some dirty martinis, which was the drink that Dean introduced me to. This time, even the vodka couldn't dull the extreme pain tearing through my heart. I kept asking myself, Why? Why? Why? I immediately called a former psychologist that had a transference issue with me as well. I had kept in touch with him the last couple of years and occasionally went in for a session or two. He said he would help me for a few sessions.

I continued drinking very heavily and was really worried about my emotional state. For the first time, I was starting to feel hopeful because Dr. Marvel agreed to see me twice weekly. But I guess that didn't last for long. No sooner than he agrees he totally pulls the plug on me. I was wondering how I would ever be able to trust a new therapist. Deep down for the very first time, I really didn't even want to look for another one. I didn't want this experience to burn me though. I was really torn in two. On one hand, I needed help, but on the other hand, I now had severe trust issues about getting that help.

I was very grateful that I still had Dr. Love's help and now I would also have Dr. Lahr's help at least for a few sessions anyway. I did therapy with Dr. Lahr for one year. But after I wrote him a "goodbye email" stating all that was wrong with him in our therapy he told me he no longer wanted me as a patient. We did have a last session and talked it over. He agreed he would see me for consultation whenever I was "in-between shrinks". This worked out well and lasted for five years. I would try to make the best of it.

I wrote Dr. Lahr in email before coming in for my session trying to explain a little of what I was going through.

Dr. Lahr,

I will see you tomorrow at 11:30. Whatever you offer me is fine. But it will be a long time until I'm even ready to look for another therapist. I could find another one quite easily.....THIS TIME THAT IS NOT THE ISSUE...........for the FIRST TIME (because of Dr. Marvel's UNETHICAL, and TRAUMATIC ENDING) I DO NOT TRUST. I must somehow work out the severe trauma that happened with Dr. Marvel FIRST....to even venture into another therapy. I am in critical condition of needing help. I am also caught in a catch-22 about getting help.

Sandy

On the drive over to his house, I was starting to have a major panic attack. This really frightened me because I can get very dizzy when I have these attacks. If I get dizzy while driving the car, I could lose control and get in an accident. I called my husband and kept him talking to me until I made it safely to Dr. Lahr's house. He too had a home office. I wasn't even sure I was going to make it because the night before I was up with excruciating menstrual cramps, diarrhea, and vomiting. I had a dizzy spell in the morning and almost passed out on the bathroom floor.

When I got to Dr. Lahr's office, he could see that I was visibly shaken. I told him I was in "panic mode" and that I spent all night violently sick. He kindly went and brought me a glass of water, moved the stand closer to the couch where I was sitting, so that I could put my glass of water down between sips.

I told him that I was in total shock over Dr. Marvels' behavior, that what he did was wrong. I even sent him an email from another psychologist who told me how to ethically end treatment. This conversation is from a psychology group that I belong to on LinkedIn. The topic was a therapist's transference. Here is what that doctor said:

Hi SANDRA, Transference is an integral component of effective therapy. From your description of the events that transpired, I can only conclude that this therapist is not trained or skilled in psychodynamic psychotherapy, so countertransference was problematic, and the therapeutic relationship was terminated in an unethical and unprofessional manner. The termination process is intense and emotionally loaded for both client and therapist. The termination phase is considered a two—person event. Appropriate termination helps avoid betrayal of the trust and abuse of power. It also prevents harm and conveys caring, a touchstone of ethical treatment.

Unfortunately, not all clients achieve this desired psychotherapy outcome.

Therapists who have had painful experiences, have confronted adversity, or have experienced physical or emotional suffering, have some degree of woundedness.

It is important to differentiate between the wounded healer and the impaired professional. The latter refers to therapists who are wounded and whose personal distress adversely impacts their clinical work. It is critical that a therapist's wounds are mostly healed, or at least understood and processed sufficiently, to prevent them from interfering with therapy and the therapeutic relationship. When therapists perceive treatment to be successful, they will have a more positive reaction to the termination. You need to be very selective in engaging future therapeutic services, by choosing a therapist who is trained, experienced and skilled in psychodynamic psychoanalysis. As mentioned by another respondent, successfully completed treatment goals will not be affected and treatment records could be transferred with your permission. Good Luck in your future endeavors.

I was trying to get some support from other professional psychologists around the world. It was helpful for me to read this one doctor's advice. I was also happy to be seeing Dr. Lahr and finally getting a chance to talk about it face to face.

Dr. Lahr talked real candidly about what he went through when I left and how it made him feel. I think he was trying to get me to see the way that I made Dr. Marvel feel. That maybe I made Dr. Marvel feel bad about his effectiveness as a therapist. I wondered what side Dr. Lahr was on! It seemed he only had compassion for Dr. Marvel and not me! Reacting that way by kicking me out of therapy is unprofessional and unethical. He should have sought his own psychological help, as he was struggling with this.

I had an ok session with Dr. Lahr. And I would be seeing both him and Dr. Love the following week. But I still felt completely abandoned and carried deep trauma over the abrupt termination of my two-year therapy with Dr. Marvel. I'm the type of person that doesn't get over hurt very easily. I still carry all the pain from my childhood inside of me. And I am sure that I will be carrying this pain with me too for a very long time.

Dr. Marvel wasn't the only therapist I had abandonment issues with. I had them as well with Dr. Love. When I first went to Dr. Love, he had these rescue hero fantasies. He tried to be "superman". He was available to me 24/7. I could call him on his vacation; wake him up in the middle of the night. He just never shut off until he burnt out. And when he did finally burn out from being superhuman shrink I felt severely abandoned. I didn't know what was happening or why he was shutting down.

Many years later we discussed the matter. He said that I was too intense and demanding, that I wanted all his time, which was true. I think when a therapeutic error has occurred it is cathartic for the therapist to own it and discuss it with the patient. This helps the healing process, by naming it and talking about the feelings that came up, not only for the patient but for the therapist as well. I really don't believe that therapy should be completely one-sided. In my opinion, certain situations beg for self-disclosure. In certain situations, self-disclosure actually *HELPS* the patient.

Me as an Alien

Alien on Deck

I'm such a clown!

Dorothy searching for Home

Me dressed for Boston Comic Con 2017

Sunshine on the water looks so lovely.

Chapter 7

My Analysis

If I could pick apart what happened I would say that Dr. Marvel was a man who had unhealed, repressed wounds and that something within me stirred those wounds up and brought them to the surface.

I think Dr. Marvel lost all his objectivity when it came to me. I think I stripped him of his armor. I also see therapy in a very different way than most people. I don't see therapy as a means to an end. I see therapy as an ongoing process of self-discovery. I see the therapist as a companion on the journey to true self. I don't agree with the complete one-sided relationship of the therapeutic bond. Yes, I do agree that the primary focus should be on the patient, but not to the exclusion that it acts as a wall of defense.

I think once the therapist starts "reacting" to the patient, once they feel provoked, it's time to talk to another professional, time to self-reflect what is going on inside of the therapist. I think it's a good idea for the therapist to let the patient know how they are feeling. The patient can see the reaction in the therapist anyway. If the patient said something hurtful, tell them "I feel hurt." If the therapist isn't feeling well in a session, they should always tell the patient. The patient will pick subtle signs that something is wrong and internalize it in themselves, feeling that they did something wrong instead.

A therapist is supposed to be able to handle all the feelings from their patient, including but not limited to loving, sexual, hateful, and jealous feelings. These feelings should be talked about openly and honestly. There should never be any taboo subjects that the patient is not allowed to talk about. The therapeutic relationship is a very deep and intimate one. There are going to be a lot of feelings that come up for both the therapist and the patient. It is the ability of the therapist to hold and manage these feelings successfully that make or break the therapy.

It is also ok for the therapist to have loving feelings for the patient and to be able to express them. The therapist can never express any sexual feelings or act on them, though.
But that doesn't mean that the therapist can't allow his loving feelings to show through. The therapeutic relationship is a restorative relationship. Most patients have wounds that they are carrying within them from previous relationships. As a therapist, you don't want to repeat that trauma. You want to heal these past scars and create a corrective experience for the patient.

I was not allowed that corrective experience with Dr. Marvel. He abruptly terminated the therapy and left me feeling abandoned.

This recently happened yet AGAIN with my long-term therapist Dr. Love. He called me during his summer vacation telling me that if I called him and left a message, he would call me back. The summer was going along fine. I even survived my Covid-19 vaccination without getting sick, as many others had. Then the unimaginable happened. It was a hot August Tuesday evening. My husband's phone rings. It turns out that it was the VP of adult services of the organization running our son's home, (where our handicapped son resides). He informed my husband that Alex was brutally beaten by a staff "supposedly watching over him". He said the police were involved.

I was in deep shock! I took the phone from my husband and started screaming at the VP. I told him that I would sue them. I told him that I had sued the Boston Public School system and won when they refused to fund a residential place for my son once he got violently sick from meningitis (please read "Life with my Schizophrenic Father"). I got a bottle of Smirnoff Vodka 100 proof and started guzzling it down, saying "I want to kill myself".

That weekend I called Dr. Love and broke down on his answering machine about what happened. He was coming home from his MONTH-LONG vacation. I must have left over a dozen messages, stating it was "an emergency". I had a major fight with my husband over this. I felt Alex was no longer safe. And I wanted to pull him out of there and take him home. But my husband refused. I contacted DDS and a lawyer. He NEVER called me back. I wrote him an email and sent a PICTURE of Alex sporting a black eye – NO RESPONSE!!

I was appalled! This wouldn't be the first time he's treated me cruelly. When I found a mass on my breast during a routine mammogram, and I needed a biopsy to check for breast cancer he callously said, "you've been through it before". I begged to take the blanket that was in his office with me for the biopsy and return it right away afterward. This blanket had special meaning to me. It was the blanket that he placed over me and tucked me in with on his couch!! He callously said, "another patient's using it". I would understand, and I think most people would of the very special circumstances of why I needed it that _one time._

He also took away one of my sessions and gave it to another patient!!! He LIED and said he had to drive his daughter to basketball practice. When I walked out, I saw the patient go into his office "at the time he was supposed to be driving his daughter". I WAS CRUSHED!! This was the time I went to the board for the SECOND time filing a complaint of his abuse. But he talked me out of it saying he gave his time for free. No matter if the patient pays Full, on a sliding scale, OR is pro bono ALL PATIENTS SHOULD BE TREATED EQUALLY AND WITH RESPECT!!!

The first session back after his vacation was the LAST session for me. After ignoring all my phone calls during the crisis of my son being brutally beaten. Also ignoring the email, I sent along with the horrible picture of Alex with a black eye I laid into him. I asked him why he never got back to me.

He slunk in his chair, facing away from me in shame. He snapped my head off and sharply said "I was busy". "I'm tied up". "I'm swamped". He NEVER once said how horrible it was that my son was beaten up. He NEVER once said that he was sorry for not getting back to me when I was in a crisis!!

After this, I ghosted him. I never officially ended the therapy. I just stopped coming and never said goodbye. It's been five months and I have NO PLANS of ever speaking to him again.
He did however write me an email after four months. Here is that email:

Sandra,

Given it's a new year, I wanted to reach out to you. It feels to me that if I can listen carefully to your criticisms and complaints and tell you what was going on with me when you tried reaching me at the end of the summer when Alex was so brutally beaten, and if you could for a few moments put aside your "psychotic rage" and revenge fantasies, we could reconnect in a way that was helpful to you. We know each other well enough so this should be possible. As you've said many times, I'm the only one who's stayed with you over the years, and I really don't want to interrupt that now. Let me know what you think.

First, when I was in session he NEVER listened to my criticisms!!! He chewed my head off instead, telling me how busy he was!!! There is _NO APOLOGY AT ALL_ for the horrific way he treated me in this email!! Also, it looks like after several months he's come up with excuses as to "what was going on with him". It doesn't matter what is "going on" with the therapist. It is their job to always be present to the patient.

Finally, in this email, he was gaslighting me. Here are the lines in which he was doing that: "if you could for a few moments put aside your "psychotic rage" and revenge fantasies". Here he is calling me crazy and full of revenge because I will no longer stand for his abuse! Shifting the blame on me and not taking any responsibility for his actions are the hallmarks of gaslighting!

Chapter 8

Dr. Lahr

I called Dr. Lahr the cowardly lion because he was afraid of taking me on as a full-time patient. Read the book "Looking For Mr. Goodshrink" for more on this relationship. He told me over and again that he was NOT my psychologist. He said instead that he was my consultant. This was highly unusual. He would only allow me to see him during the transitional phase from one therapist to another. So, when one therapy ended, we could get together for a session and talk about that failure before I found someone else for their replacement. And always as we talked, he would solely focus on what I could do better the next time, to prevent another rupture with yet another psychologist.

After five years of being my consultant, coupled with the fact that I failed to produce another therapist he ended that role as well and cut me off completely!!! Another psychologist kicking me to the curb! Except this one wasn't in the role as my therapist, only a consultant. I was still, nonetheless upset and felt abandoned once again.

Dr. Lahr also saw Dean and me for couple's therapy! That would make Dean (my former psychologist turned lover – read the book "Love Outside The Boundaries") be in therapy with not one but TWO of my other psychologists! If that isn't crazy, I don't know what is!!!

For one year as Dr. Lahr's patient, we did alright. I covered up the fact that I was borderline. Most psychologists don't like borderlines. And furthermore, most can't handle them without the transference getting in the way.

Countertransference is when the psychologist reacts toward the patient. If the psychologist gets angry or frustrated and takes it out on the patient that is wrong. A good psychologist should not take anything the patient says personally. Rather, they should question what the patient is going through and feeling. If the psychologist gets triggered by the patient, they will act defensively and lose their objectivity. When this happens, the therapy goes down the drain.

As a borderline, I could not regulate my feelings. It is like a broken thermostat, either boiling hot or frigid cold. I was either idolizing/in love with my therapist or devaluing them. Dr. Lahr could not handle my criticism. He got triggered by it. People get triggered in the present by relationships they had in the past. It brings up old wounds. So, when I criticized Dr. Lahr it reminded him of his father, who was an alcoholic and belittled him and beat him. For him to tell me this was self-disclosure. I should not have known this. It served no purpose in my therapy.

So, when I finally told Dr. Lahr what I thought about him in a "goodbye email" that was it. He did not ask me to come in and talk about it. He just let me go.

Here is that email, marking the last of our relationship as therapist and patient (before he became my consultant)

Dear Sandy

As I have suggested to you at times, I think it is often best not to respond quickly, with one's immediate reactions to events such as your email of a few days ago, so I wanted to let things settle, and I also thought it was possible that you would decide to attend on Tuesday for further discussion. But in the email age, that now seems redundant. I did have difficulty with your accusatory tone and the liberties that you took in expressing your judgments of me, though I certainly knew more abstractly that you would be prone to that type of behavior when feeling let down. I know that you yourself have had all too much of the experience of being spoken to disrespectfully, and of course your past experiences of feeling abandoned, ignored, etc are part of what came up for you. At this point, I do think it best for me to accept your decision to terminate. As you and Dean have found, relationships (of various kinds) can be tough, and not all obstacles can be fixed.

I want to say that I have never knowingly spoken to you with disrespect. I don't recall what I said that felt dismissive to you, but I certainly regret that you ceased to experience our sessions as well enough attuned to your needs.

Your input in the first email suggests that it was really not at all good for you that, when you've picked up that something was weighing on me, I acknowledged first the death of our dog and then the fact that I had just been facing a difficult clinical challenge with another patient. As you say, I have at times reacted as a person, and not only in my professional role; one strives to maintain clinical perspective, but I don't know anyone who achieves that standard in every case. I will take your comments to heart as I pay attention to my own in-session stance and treatment decisions. Please focus on yourself and don't worry about your views of my issues as you move forward.

You have moved on from previous therapists when you needed to, and I now join their ranks. At times like this, like that previous occasion on which you fired me, it is good to know that you you're your longstanding primary therapy with Dr. Love to rely on. And I know that you are extremely adept at finding and evaluating potential therapists. I think that we did have a fairly extended period of productive therapy together. Among other things, you have found that you have been able to dramatically reduce your drinking when motivated to do so, which was the issue that initially brought you to see me. Now that we have reached an impasse, I hope that you can remember some of the positive moments (as I will) once you move on to what I'm sure will be further useful work on yourself.

I was shocked that he went along with my "flying off the handle" goodbye email!!! It is customary to ask the patient to come in for the last session and talk about it. Here is another time I flew off the handle with my psychologist and "ended the treatment" by email. This is the appropriate response a therapist should make after having received such an email:

Sandra,

I'm sorry that you are feeling hurt by what I had revealed...and am concerned about how you are interpreting it and now refusing to speak. In many ways, I believe I can understand and appreciate why you are feeling hurt, but I fear that it is ultimately based in a misreading of the situation, which I am appealing to you to allow us at least the chance to address! I am concerned that you are blending or identifying the type of connection, care and love that has emerged in our relationship with a relationship in my personal life that is of a totally different sort. One has no real bearing on the other...and needn't in any way be a diminishment of or a threat to what exists between us! What you have stated in the past is that you believed that if I became involved with someone in my personal life that our relationship would end because I would lose interest in you and not care for or love you anymore!

I challenged that contention over and again...and assert even more strongly now in this instance that it is not in any sense what has been happening...and I believe would never happen because of the nature of the unique bond that we share.

And the holding of you all along has come out of that bond, out of that deep place of connection, care and love...which we have both said over and again has been very real and true and more meaningful and healing than any mere romantic embrace...and I can't help but think that at some level you still know that to be true!

And I don't understand how I possibly could have used you through IFS. Because it has had personal value for me in addressing the challenges that have come up in our work together, I have wanted to share and use the model with you and to enable you the benefits of it as well...my wish to utilize it in our work going forward has come totally out of my desire to help you and has not in any way been about a using of you!

I will not fill the slot on Tuesday, and I am again appealing to you Sandra to please re-consider this and allow us to address this situation together in person! Given what we have had and can still have, I believe it would truly be a tragedy to end our work and relationship in this way without even the chance of an opportunity to make sure that it is really well founded and truly the right or necessary thing to do!

A therapist is supposed to have a corrective/restoring and healing effect on the patient. They are not supposed to react as a friend or relation would. Most patients will come into therapy treating the therapist as they do other people in their life. It's the therapist's job to have the therapy not end up as the past relationships that were damaging to the patient. If this happens it further sets back the patient, as the psychologist and therapy become another traumatic experience instead of a restorative, healing one.

Chapter 9

After 16 Years of Therapy

I wrote a LinkedIn article comparing my life before therapy (actually before my long-term therapy with Dr. Love) and life after my therapy. Here is that article:

OMNIPOTENT NARCISSISTIC MEN SHOULD NOT DO THERAPY!!! Before Dr. Love I had NO ALCOHOL problem. Maybe had a beer or two with pizza on the weekend. I had friends and socialized often, throwing parties, or going to parties at friends' homes. I never stole a thing! I never sold my body doing porn! Then as I turned 40 EVERYTHING CHANGED!!! This man told me I needed therapy 5 hours a week!!! He gave this for free because insurance wouldn't pay for more than 1 session a week. At first, he tried to bill it through his wife - which is unethical and violates HIPAA (as I am NOT a patient of his wife) He told me I could call him 24/7. He even called me when he was on "his vacation" This man sang to me on the floor James Taylor's song "You've got a friend" on a Sunday. I sat in his lap!!! laid over him on his lap and grabbed his penis. Stripped TOTALLY NAKED for him WHILE HE WATCHED!!! And then he wrote a paper about it and gave a speech!!! He told me intimate details of his life, like when his wife had breast cancer. And that they had sex outside by the lake in Maine. He told me about his stillborn sibling, and how his mother suffered a deep depression.

And then it stopped! He said I was too intense for him. He made promises he didn't keep. I fell apart and turned to alcohol. He was no longer available 24/7. He NEVER returned my calls. He cut back the therapy and pulled away physically. I felt abandoned ALL OVER AGAIN, like in my childhood being raised with a paranoid schizophrenic father! I turned to other psychologists who told me that this man was responsible for all my problems. I left therapy. I went to the board twice, only to rescind the complaints because I was "hooked on him" like a drug!!! When I came back, he only gave me 10 minutes sessions!!! He gradually increased it to 30 minutes after I begged him for years!! He told me he didn't want me!!

This man saw the psychologist I was having sex with for two years and I TOGETHER FOR COUPLES COUNSELLING, encouraging an abusive/sexual/UNETHICAL relationship with another psychologist! I had to always have a second psychologist since he refused to give me a NORMAL "50 MINUTE SESSION". He even took that psychologist on as his own patient and defended his behavior!!!!

Still, he's OUT THERE charging $300.00 an hour!!! As I'm drinking 4 vodka martini drinks and having severe stomach pains. I lost all my friends and became a kleptomaniac in my fifties. Beware of omnipotent shrinks who think they are GOD and prey on damsels in distress! Beware of shrinks that seem too good to be true and promise you the moon - then when you need them, they are nowhere to be found. I called him when I read the report about my severely handicap son being brutally beaten by a staff member in charge of his care.

He was punched in the stomach and sporting a black eye, tormented, and teased unmercifully!!! HE IGNORED MY CRIES FOR HELP!!!! This was the same person that called me from airports AT MIDNIGHT waking my husband and me up out of a sound sleep!! I am devastated beyond repair. This man PROTECTED the psychologist who had sex with me!! He took him as his own patient and refused to tell me the truth about him!

Here is the T graph I made of life Before my therapy and life After

B.T.	A.T.
had close friends	no friends
a beer once a week	4 vodka drinks a DAY
never stole	became a kleptomaniac
never did porn	sold my body for money on OF
socialized/partied	complete hermit/never talks
bought a house	neglected home and family
had boundaries	had sex with psychologist

I deeply regret seeing him. He has made my life a living hell!

I write books and articles like these to enlighten people about the dangers of therapy and psychologists. I don't mean to scare people off from getting the help they need. But patients should have their eyes wide open and trust their gut instinct when they start therapy.

Unfortunately for me, therapy had become yet another traumatic experience piled on top of all the ones I already had when I started in the first place. None of my therapies ended mutually or were restorative and healing for me. They became new wounds. I carry new scars from them. I've turned into an alcoholic over them.

The worst one of all was my sexual affair with one psychologist that lasted two years. Sex is NEVER allowed in therapy. It is never allowed to end the treatment to engage in a sexual relationship with a patient. You cannot be a patient's friend or lover and do therapy. What made this situation even worse is that the psychologist was also seeing my long-term one as his patient as well. So, neither one of them was protecting me!!

When a psychologist sees a patient, they should not take on that patient's lover/friend or family. This one (Dr. Love) took on an unethical psychologist who was abusing me as his patient, leaving me to feel all alone and unprotected. I did ask him to see him, in the beginning giving up my own sessions to allow it. But what the patient wants isn't always in their best interest. A child might want to stay up all night and eat junk food. It is up to the parent to set the boundary. Just as it is up to the psychologist to set up the boundary with the patient. It is always the responsibility of the therapist to uphold those boundaries.

It is very confusing when you set up the therapy one way and then abruptly change it. A therapist needs to maintain consistency throughout the therapy. My therapy with Dr. Love was completely inconsistent. It retraumatized me. When I was a child, my father was inconsistent. He would turn on and off like a light switch. He suffered from schizophrenia. He would be calming and nice one minute. The next minute who would be a raving maniac. He was more like Jekyll and Hyde than what a real father should be.

In the beginning of treatment, Dr. Love would send me emails like this one when he was on his summer vacation:

Dear Sandy,

Yes, vacation is enjoyable, and it is peaceful by
the lake and you're right about the morning sun.
Swimming, kayaking, running so far. Yesterday while
kayaking saw a baby loon with its parents, which is
rare because it is difficult for baby loons to survive
these days with all the raccoons looking for food. They
ride on their parents back until they learn to swim.
Otherwise just enjoying nature and settling in.

I agree with your "Who are you..." email. Just have
to get the rest of the shrink world to go along too.
Speaking of which, I hope tomorrow goes well. Let me
know. In any case, will call you Thursday morning. Am
thinking of you also and hope things are going well.

This email is something that "a friend" would send, blurring the boundaries of the therapy. He once sang that song by James Taylor "You've got a friend" while sitting close to me on the floor during a Sunday afternoon. Later, he would stop sending me emails like this. In fact, he would downright stop responding to my emails altogether, making me feel abandoned.

He would allow me to call him any time of the day or night, on the weekends and during his vacation. Then he abruptly stopped that as well. One Saturday evening he left his wife sitting alone in a restaurant while he flirted with me on the phone. When he got back to his house after the dinner, he called back again, only to continue the flirting.

To prove to myself that he still loved me I asked to see him one Saturday after he got back from his long flight from his in-laws. He reluctantly agreed to it. I told him I wanted to go to the park with him. It was a warm, sunny spring day in April. He said that I didn't "really need to see him". But I pleaded, and he relented. I never used to have to plead to see him before and I felt deeply crushed. But I convinced myself that he must still love me because he was willing to see me on a Saturday just for fun, knowing I was ok and not of any need for psychological help.

I drove to his house with the windows cranked all the way down to catch the warm breeze and had the radio blaring loud. I was happy as a lark! I was seeing the man I loved and going to the park.

I brought my son's football for us to toss around. When I arrived, I sat crisscrossed on his neighbor's tree stump and waited for him to come out of his house.

I didn't want to ring his door and disturb his family. He came out unshaven, unkempt, wearing sunglasses and black jeans and sneakers.

He was sporting this Cheshire cat smile as if he was very happy to see me.

We proceeded to walk to a nearby park in his neighborhood. When we got there, we tossed the football around. It was a busy day at the park. There was a baseball game going on nearby and children were playing on the swings and playground equipment. After we got done playing catch, we laid on the grass. He laid completely down with is elbows stretched out and hands entwined behind his head. I started swirling a blade of the fresh green grass of early spring. I went to touch him, and he said, "not here". Of course, people knew him there. He was on his own turf. We just stayed like that, no words.

Soon after this he took away my therapy and gave it to another patient. He stopped all outside contact as well. He also would not respond to me in times of crisis.

Chapter 10

My Search for Therapists

This was yet another failed attempt with a psychologist who already had one patient bring them before the licensing board. This is from my book "Looking for Mr. Goodshrink"

I was excited to see Dr. Radeb. He was genuine and kind and had a great personality, not to mention he was cute too! I sat on his long couch, and he took the chair across from the large, glass top coffee table. He also was a music person. He had a piano and guitar in his living room like the last few psychologists I've seen. It seems these days that a lot of psychologists are musically inclined. I liked this guy's living room, with the white walls and skylight windows. It was bright and airy. I did find it strange that he had no office. He just conducted therapy in his living room. He offered to make me tea during the session! The kitchen was opened to the living room.

I continued from the last session telling him more about my past with my other psychologists, and about my childhood. He said, "You have a problem with men." He acknowledged my traumatic childhood, saying that I grew up with no boundaries. My father was a paranoid schizophrenic, in and out of mental hospitals all my life. And my mother would blame me for making her life hard when I got really frightened by his psychotic rages.

Dr. Radeb was the first psychologist to notice me dissociating in the session. Suddenly my face would change and although I was physically in the room with him my spirit had left my body and wandered off somewhere. He asked me where it went, but I couldn't answer him. He jokingly said that when I figured it out my spirit would send him "a postcard" from whatever place it had visited.

I finally broke down and told him that I am still seeing Dr. Love. He thought this was "weird" having two psychologists. He said it was "splitting." And that it would be very confusing having two different opinions. But I told him that Dr. Love mainly just listened and didn't offer advice. And that I was never confused all these years of having two psychologists. I knew that if I wanted to go forward with Dr. Radeb I would have to be honest with him, even though it was a HUGE risk.

It didn't deter him from making a third appointment with me. I was still very scared about whether he would change his mind by then. Dr. Badeb did say that I was unusual. But I don't want to be ordinary! Many psychologists before him had said the exact same thing! He also thought that I was psychic because I told him the time that I predicted that Dr. Marvel had prostate cancer, and I was correct. He said I was intuitive. Others have said that about me too. But no one ever called me "psychic." I told him that I feared having this ability because there are some things I just don't want to know about ahead of time.

That night I woke up in a sweat with heart palpitations. This worried me because my mother died of heart failure, and so did my former lover, Dean. I knew that my drinking was out of hand. I just needed something to hold onto, some stability.

I was so scared that Dr. Radeb would be like the others before him and let me down. And after all, I have been actively searching for two months. I thought that if this fell through, I would be in a very sorry place. I was very scared for myself.

I had my session with Dr. Love today. I told him that I was worried that Dr. Radeb was going to tell me on Wednesday that he couldn't see me anymore because I was seeing him. I confessed that I need much more help than the free forty-minute sessions Dr. Love was giving me once a week. I said that after two whole months of actively looking and drinking very heavily since Dr. Marvel kicked me out of therapy. If it fell through with Dr. Radeb I was really worried about myself both psychically and mentally.

Dr. Love should have seen that I needed more therapy and the great lengths I was going through to get it. It felt like he was punishing me because I left therapy when he treated me badly. That is why he gave me the reduced time. Every time I brought it up he snapped "You left".

Today I walked into my appointment with Dr. Radeb with trepidation and a poem! I haven't been sleeping well at night because I awakened with a racing heart. And I've had dizzy spells all during the day. This is the poem

"I'm In Pieces"

I'm in pieces.
A part of me is over there,
another one is floating in the air.
There's one that someone took.
One's still on the hook.
There's one shattered so bad
it's nowhere to be had.
There's one that's totally gone,
another that's hanging on.
What did you ever do
with the one I gave to you?

Dr. Radeb liked the poem! He told me he has published poems himself! He didn't say a word about my seeing Dr. Marvel. I told him that I was terrified of him throwing me out the door. He said, "I'll hold a big sign up that says, "I won't fire you." We both laughed. Then he started asking me questions that sounded very contrived. He was looking at a sheet of paper while he was doing this. I answered them, though it felt like he was reading off some list. I told him it felt like I was in a repair shop, and he was the repairman going to "fix me" and then send me on my way.

I started stressing out and moved to the far end of the couch. He said what he was doing was "CBT therapy" with me.

I told him that I didn't like it. It felt contrived. So, he stopped. Then I opened up and confessed more about of my past to him, which included going to the licensing board over Dean and taking legal action. I also mentioned the other psychologists that I made formal complaints to the board to as well.

I could see that he was getting very uptight upon hearing this news. He told me that he didn't feel safe with me. I told him that I was a "borderline" also and asked him if he ever worked with any borderlines before. He got defensive and said, "I've been doing this for thirty-seven years." He couldn't just answer a simple "yes?"

He said that he would need to draw up a "contract" for me to sign stating I would never go to the licensing board over him. He also said that he needed to "talk to someone else about this". This didn't sound too promising to me. He told me he would see me next week. He also told me that this made him feel unsafe and queasy, and that going to the board would be like "ripping his heart out". I told him "I want you to feel safe." I also said that I would do whatever that took to make him feel that way. And that I respected him if he decided he didn't want to see me. When I asked my husband if he thought I was sabotaging myself he said, "you're just being honest."
This time it felt truly different. I always thought of myself as "Dorothy" from the Wizard of Oz, looking for home. But now "home" was some abstract concept. And all the key players were gone. I didn't know if Dr. Radeb would continue to see me, since he said that I made him feel queasy. I didn't know anything anymore, except my honesty kept getting me in trouble.

But I didn't know how to do therapy without being honest. And frankly, I really didn't want to do it any other way.

I was a high-risk patient, no doubt. Not too many patients take their therapist to the board. I had taken three!! The first psychologist I took to the board was a very old narcissistic man. He thought he had me wrapped around his stubby pinky. He arrogantly told me during one session: "I can treat you like SHIT and you won't leave because you're hooked on me". Not only did I leave him, but I made a formal complaint to the licensing board for psychologists. They investigated; but dropped it, unfortunately.

The second complaint I made was to the licensing board of social workers. I was seeing this ugly, fat social worker in a clinic a few minutes from my house. I didn't have insurance. And he only charged me $20.00 for an hour session.

He was always asking me inappropriate questions, like what kind of vibrator I used. Then he went into great detail of all the different kinds of vibrators out on the market, like the kind with the little tickly head!!!!! I told him to STOP asking me inappropriate questions! Really! I never mentioned masturbation to him. So why was he bringing up vibrators!?! But the last straw came when he tried to engage me in having phone sex with him. I was on the phone crying my eyes out about Dr. Love not seeing me anymore and he asked: "How close are you to cuming right now on a scale of one through ten, an eight"?

That was the last straw for me. I do not know for the life of me how one can associate crying with sexual excitement. The next morning after that phone call I made the complaint. But he was already in hot water with the board. One of the board's lawyers told me (on the sly) that he was practicing therapy out of his home without a proper license. After two years of investigations, and a trial date already picked he surrendered his license to practice therapy anymore. And that was the end of him.

The third person I took to the board was the psychologist I had a two-year sexual affair with. Of course, they prosecuted him. But he died before anything happened. I always felt responsible for his death. I also got a lawyer and went after him legally.

There was also a fourth person I made TWO separate complaints to the licensing board, spread two years apart. That was Dr. Love. I rescinded both complaints. They never even got acknowledged by the board. But I had formally written both out and mailed them.

The first time I did it was because Dr. Love's "care" was over the top for me. I just couldn't handle the extreme closeness. He saw me for FREE five hours a week. He would allow me to call him in the middle of the night. I could sit in his lap and lie on the floor with him. There wasn't much he wouldn't let me do. When he abruptly stopped being "super shrink" I was left feeling extremely abandoned.

So, I had quite a colorful past with therapists. It's no wonder why most were scared to take me on as their patient! At the same time as well, I started having romantic feelings for Dr. Radeb. I had only known him for a month now. But the informal setting of doing therapy in his living room, knowing he was divorced (from his timeline on Facebook), and his great sense of humor and rugged good looks kept him pretty much in my head for most of the day, not to mention the nighttime as well.

We had our first snowfall of the year over the weekend. It was cold and everything was covered in white on this early sunny, Monday morning. I was headed over to Dr. Love's office with Dr. Radeb firmly fixated in my mind. I walked into Dr. Love's office confessing my feelings of attraction (AGAIN for another shrink) and my extreme fear of being abandoned at the same time.

As I was talking, I noticed something fall out of Dr. Love's pocket and hit the ground with a thump. It was a pocketknife. Well, what do you know! I never knew Dr. Love would be the type to carry a knife around with him. He looked and acted just like Mr. Rogers, from the children's program I watched following Sesame Street growing up, on public television of course, where there are no commercials!

Dr. Love didn't know what Dr. Radeb would do as far as keeping me as a patient or "throwing me out the door." But he said that I had changed and that I wouldn't go to the board anymore. He also said that he would speak to Dr. Radeb on the phone if he didn't believe this. He said that I should tell him that I had changed, that therapy had helped me to become less psychotic. But he was clueless. I hadn't changed at all! I was using large volumes of alcohol to suppress my rage instead. But Dr. Love didn't care!   He couldn't handle my rage.

The day before my appointment was one of the scariest of my life. I almost passed out at the Laundromat from a severe dizzy spell. I was doing my nails at the time and spilled purple nail polish all over my pants from losing control. I was worried sick about getting in the car and driving after that. My aunt died from a brain tumor at my age. My mind started racing that I had one as well. I just couldn't go on without getting the help I so desperately needed.

The day of the appointment I felt like a severe panic attack was coming on when I was taking a bath. I was scared shit. I thought, oh great! What happens if I faint in a bathtub filled to the brim with water? I'll drown for sure. To reassure myself I had to repeat the few things I had that were secure in my life. I said repeatedly out loud: Andrew (my husband) Austin (my youngest son) Alex (my oldest) and vodka (my crutch). Somehow this helped me get through taking a bath without fainting.

When I got to Dr. Radeb's office his previous patient was coming out with a wide-ass grin on. That's good customer service if I don't say so myself! Radeb had me come in. I took off my coat. No sooner than I sat down I noticed the music sheet that was opened on his piano. It had the notes to the Neil Diamond song "Song Sung Blue."

Radeb didn't mention last week and how he said it made him
feel queasy that I went to the licensing board so many times.
I handed him the co-pay and a new poem I wrote this week.
Here is that poem:

"You've Got the Cure"

I'm a flat, misshapen piece of rubber.
Breathe air into me; won't you fly this balloon?
I'm meat that's laden with blubber.
I need a trim sometime real soon.
I'm an ignitable wick embedded in wax.
Won't you please be so kind as to be my match?
I'm an empty wall filled with hairline cracks.
I think I'm in need of a good patch.
I'm a flimsy kite tied to a string.
You're tough and strong; won't you be my wind?
I'm a lonely, rusty, old backyard swing.
Give me a push,
and I'll be all yours.
I'm an infectious disease, doctor.
And you've got the cure.

He didn't look at it. He laid it on the coffee table, as I began
to talk about my dizzy spell and just how wound uptight, I
was.

He asked me why I didn't take medication to control the anxiety. I told him I had a life-threatening allergic reaction to Motrin in my thirties that left me paralyzed with fear of taking any medicine at all. Drinking alcohol became my own way to medicate myself. When I feel like I'm crawling out of my skin (which seems to be every day now) a couple of drinks will calm me right down.

I also mentioned to Radeb about getting totally naked for Dr. Love. And I told him Dr. Love wrote a paper about the incident and gave me a copy of it. He told me to bring the paper in so he could read it. He also told me that he too had a female patient that took her clothes off for him. He told me that he left the room when she did that. When he later returned, he told her "You can't do that." He asked what Dr. Love did when I stripped for him. I said "nothing"; he just stayed there and watched!!

We then went on talking about my affair with Dean. I told him of the night I drove drunk to his house and got in a horrible car crash. I had mixed eggnog, which already had plenty of booze in it with vodka. Then I stupidly got in the car and went straight to Dean's house, feeling no pain. It was only a short ten-minute drive there. But that's all it took to crash head-on to this black woman's car. I didn't stop either. I continued right on to Dean's house with her following me in her banged-up car with the front end almost falling off. This was when I was still Dean's patient before I became his lover.

When we got there, she had called the police. Before they came, I got out of my car. My car didn't have a scratch on it!! Her car was a very different story. I apologized to her. I told her that I had a doctor's appointment that I had to get to. After all, Dean was a Doctor of Psychology.

When the police came, they didn't question me or ask me to get out of the car. I thought that was extremely odd. A cop did come over to my car. I rolled down the window. He poked his head through and said to me: "You are supposed to stop at the scene of an accident." "If that woman pressed charges, I would have had to put you in jail". That was scary shit, hearing this. I never drove drunk again!

I also told Radeb how I, the patient, had regressed Dean down to a child-like state. I came in my therapy session once carrying a blue quilt and a stuffed toy tiger. I had Dean lie on the floor with me and hold the stuff tiger in his lap. He never had anything soft to hold as a child. That's when he told me that his father beat him severely. His mother made him wait all day on his knees, on a hard wooden floor for his father to get home for the beating. That alone is mental cruelty.

I told Radeb that people stop growing emotionally and become stunted at the age they were abused. I told him that if they are loved and nurtured unconditionally at the level where they got stunted, they can grow from there. I told him that's what Dr. Love tried to do with me.

It reminded me of the session when I sat beside Dr. Love on the couch. I got all the stuffed animals in the children's section of his office and put them on the couch with us, including Rudolph the red-nosed reindeer that I had given to him. We sat there among all the stuffed animals together. I felt so secure in his love. I had never experienced anything like this in my life. It's not the sort of thing that a psychologist would do with an adult patient.

I was feeling rather confident after this session with Radeb that it would work out with him. I told him right before I left that I thought he was a cool shrink and that I was lucky that I had met him. Now I had printed up a copy of his picture and was carrying it around with me. It was like Dr. Love had said that I have "relationships in my head" with people that soothe and comfort me during times of stress. But despite this comfort, I still felt like I was headed for a nervous breakdown.

My anxiety was at an all-time high. I couldn't even face people; my social phobia was that crippling. All-day long it felt like I was literally crawling out of my skin. I had printed up a copy of the "strip paper" that Dr. Love had written to bring to my next appointment with Radeb. I also printed up a copy of the poem "Madness Is" to give him as well.

Maybe this poem would explain to Radeb just how badly I
was feeling.

"Madness Is"

Screaming
with your sound turned all the way down.
Standing
in an inch of water when you drown.
Sleeping
upright during the middle of the day.
Looking
at the sun and only seeing grey.
Hearing
scary voices that are definitely not yours.
Pretending
you can vaporize to get through locked doors.
Picking
off the mites that are crawling beneath your skin.
Bleeding
to feel alive, when you stick yourself with pins.
Wrestling
with the demons that hide under your bed.
Choking
on the rhetoric that fills your empty head.

I was in a tizzy even before I entered Radeb's office. I started pacing back and forth as soon as I entered the room. My boots were making a loud clicking sound on his hard wooden floor, so I took them off. He told me that maybe I should go to McLean's (a mental hospital in Belmont). I told him I was a "visitor" there when my father was admitted. I remembered the white fireplaces in each patient's room. He said that all the celebrities went there and that the meals were good.

He constantly brought up the similarities of Dean and my dad. Dean would be hot/cold like my dad. I noticed the music on his piano again, Sung, Song Blue, by Neil Diamond. I started to sing the song as I paced around his couch. I wondered if he would play it for me. He said that he wouldn't because he wasn't very good at it. Then I noticed that he had one of my favorite pieces "Moon River" by Henry Mancini. I immediately identified it with the movie "Breakfast at Tiffany's." I began to sing that too. He said I have a nice voice.

Then I jumped over to the rocking chair in the far-left corner of his living room. I started to rock, wildly. He asked, "do you know what age you look like now?" I said, "five years old". He agreed my guess was right. I asked why he wouldn't talk about the last shrink that dumped me after two years of therapy. He couldn't give an answer but pondered that for a while.

I was getting upset that he would throw my father in my face again and again. He kept telling me just how horrible my dad was to me because he frightened me when he flew into his delusional psychotic rages. But I tried to explain that my dad

couldn't help his mental illness of schizophrenia. He was a
good father to me when he was on his medication. Radeb
was starting to get under my skin about this. I didn't know
just where he was going with this talk about my dad. No
other therapist had done this before to me.

I told him Radeb he was a hypocrite talking about my dad
and his on/off relationship with me when I had read on
Facebook that he himself was estranged from his own
daughter. He looked very sad at my mentioning this. I know I
was taking a great risk in telling him what I read. But I did
read that his daughter attended the divorce hearing with his
ex-wife, and he didn't recognize her. He thought she was his
wife's lawyer. This upset his daughter greatly. How could
her own father not even recognize her????

That abruptly put a stop to our talk about "dad". Before I left
Radeb said that we would start doing "twice a week therapy"
after the New Year. He wished me a "Merry Christmas" upon
leaving. I asked if he was Jewish, He answered "yes." I said
that I go for older Jewish shrinks.

The more I thought about it the more Radeb reminded me of a hammerhead shark. I thought that over the weekend while looking for some toy for Alex for Sunday, I would also look for a toy hammerhead shark to give to Radeb during my next session. I usually get Alex some toy animal when he comes home for dinner on Sundays. He really looks forward to it. Alex will always be at the emotional age of two. He's been like that since he got meningitis at age four.

 I went to Bertucci's, our usual Saturday night haunt. We were eating dinner when suddenly Dr. Radeb and his date walk through the door! I had already bought the hammerhead shark that I was going to give him on Wednesday when I had my therapy session with him. It was in my pocketbook.

I told my husband Andrew that I saw him, and that I was going to go up to him and give him the shark. He strongly suggested that I didn't do that. But how could I resist? He was in my Bertucci's, after all, NOT the one in his neighborhood!! So, I ran up to his table, told his date that I was his patient, and that I was sitting at the bar with my husband. I slid him the toy hammerhead shark. Told him that I was going to give it to him on Wednesday, but since he was there, I decided to do it now. Of course, he was polite and said "Hi, how are you?" I can only imagine how he will respond on Wednesday when I see him!

When I got back home, I called Dr. Love and told him about running into Dr. Radeb at the restaurant while he was on a date. His date looked mousy. She was short, old, and had thin wispy grey/brown hair. She also wore glasses. I always pictured him with a tall young blonde. I told Dr. Love about giving Radeb the hammerhead shark.

The next morning, I couldn't resist writing Radeb another email, after running into him the previous night. I know he didn't like me sending him emails, but I just had to explain why I handed him a hammerhead shark at the restaurant. And of course, the poet in me had to write a poem about it. Here it is:

Dr. Radeb,

I usually go to Bertucci's every Saturday with my husband. I already had the hammerhead shark in my pocketbook keeping the pig company that I bought for Alex (my brain-damaged son) when he comes up for dinner on Sunday. I always get him some toys. I couldn't resist giving it to you, instead of waiting until Wednesday. I called Dr. Love last night and told him about our run-in! Here is the poem that goes with it. There is a lot of truth in what I do/write, but always intended with good humor and fun!!!!! So, hope you don't take offense. I think this belongs to the "Sledgehammer" one.

"Hammerhead"

His flattened head runs long, dear.
Those eyes extend wide, from side to side.
He can see right through into you;
there's never any place to hide.

Oh, the great white has such fame, dear,
but don't get fooled by this one, no siree!
He will prod you with his cephalofoil,
a slick one with the chick's hon, is he.

He will turn you over from top to bottom,
three-hundred and sixty degrees.
He can see above and below the water,
They should call him "king of the seas".

When he comes near, better run dear.
He can turn the water red from baby blue.
Those electro receptors are very strong,
and they're pointing right at the heart of you!

To my surprise, and horror quite frankly I got an email in
return from Radeb that was rather disturbing. Here it is:

Sandy,

Notwithstanding your flattery, you are skating on very thin
ice with me. I asked you not to e-mail me, and I meant it.
You said you've done DBT and so you understand acting out,
intrusive boundary-breaking behaviors and know how to
deal with them. Please review your DBT workbook and we
will do the same....Dr. Radeb

After receiving this email, I was in an intense state of panic. I started drinking heavily again. The next day my husband had to drive me for hours in the car like a newborn baby to relieve the extreme anxiety. I couldn't even stand up! I wrote Dr. Love and Dr. Lahr telling them both that Radeb was no good. Here is that email:

Dr. Love & Dr. Lahr –

Reasons why Dr. Radeb is NO GOOD

1. He has his own agenda/doesn't follow the patient's lead
2. He comes down like a sledgehammer, despite the patient's increased fear.
3. He threatens abandonment when the patient gives him an unwanted email.
4. He refuses contact between sessions
5. When the patient has an anxiety attack, he doesn't try to calm them; he escalates it

If that wasn't enough, I posted on LinkedIn about my problem as well. I said in a post "My psychologist is giving me a nervous breakdown" Over 13,000 people read the post and over one hundred replied with comments. It's always nice to know that people care. Maybe there was a reason why I was having intense anxiety since seeing Radeb, at least my husband thought so.

The next session when I walked into Radeb's office it was clear something was wrong. He said that he could no longer do therapy with me. He was too worried that I might report him to the board. He told me that he was already reported to the board by a husband of a couple he was seeing. He said that it was very costly getting a lawyer for the case. The husband became pushy with Radeb, and shoved into him at the trial telling him "he was going to pay for what he did."

The emotional impact it had on him was sustaining. He was clearly triggered. He sat there nervously wringing his hands as if they were a soaked washcloth and he was trying to get every last drop of water out of it. He jumped out of his chair twenty minutes early. He was that uncomfortable. I told him to sit back down; the session wasn't over yet. But it was clear it became intolerable for him to continue. So, I got up and left.

He was the very LAST therapist I sought after. I gave up looking for a new one. I realized that therapy wasn't for me. It wasn't for lack of trying on my part. It was because all the therapists that I saw had too many internal injuries and transference issues that they harmed me instead of helping me get better.

Although therapy didn't work out for me, I never want to discourage anyone who needs help not to seeking it. There can be some professional psychologists out there that really do help people. I hope that reading this book has provided both therapist and patient with the signs of transference and burnout and personal unresolved internal injuries of the therapist that in turn harm the patient if they get triggered in the therapy.

About The Author

Sandra Wyllie started writing in her late forties. She believes in following her dreams no matter how old you are or at what point you are in your life. She loves writing poetry, drawing, and nature. She is a big believer that one should never be too serious in life; enjoy laughing and having fun, being creative and exploring, and never putting limits on yourself.

She has been formally published in Ibbetson St. and Oddball magazines. She has written dozens of poetry books as well as psychology books all available on Amazon. Be sure to read "Life With My Schizophrenic Father" and "Love Outside The Boundaries" and "Looking For Mr. Goodshrink"

She has two sons; one has special needs. Her special needs son has taught her to enjoy the silly antics of a squirrel eating an acorn, purple flowers by the side of the road, and even the green grass growing lazily on a Sunday morning. Life is how you look at it. Look at it with love and joy and with wonder. See it through the eyes of a child.